CAT
ANTS

First, we looked at some glass tanks.
We wanted to make a tank
into an **aquarium** for our turtle.

A lot of the tanks were too little.
Some were too big!
Mum liked the long tank
because it had a lid.

After that, we got some big stones
to put in the tank.
Our turtle could sit on the stones.

A Home for Tiny Turtle

By Elsie Nelley
Illustrations by Elizabeth Botté

On Saturday,
Mum and I went to a pet shop.

We had always wanted
a little turtle for a pet.

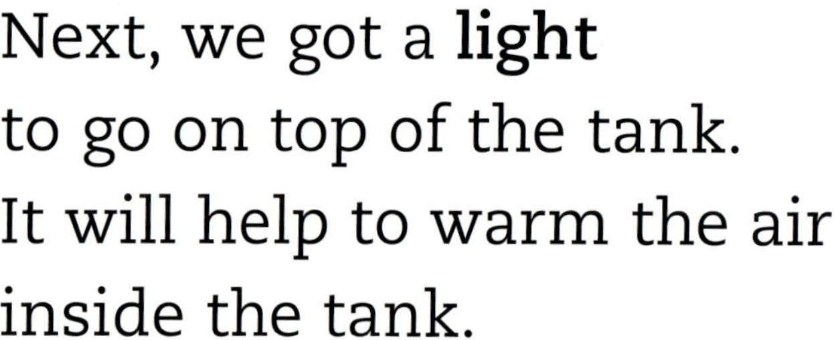

Next, we got a **light**
to go on top of the tank.
It will help to warm the air
inside the tank.

We got a small **heater**, too.
Turtles like to swim in warm water.

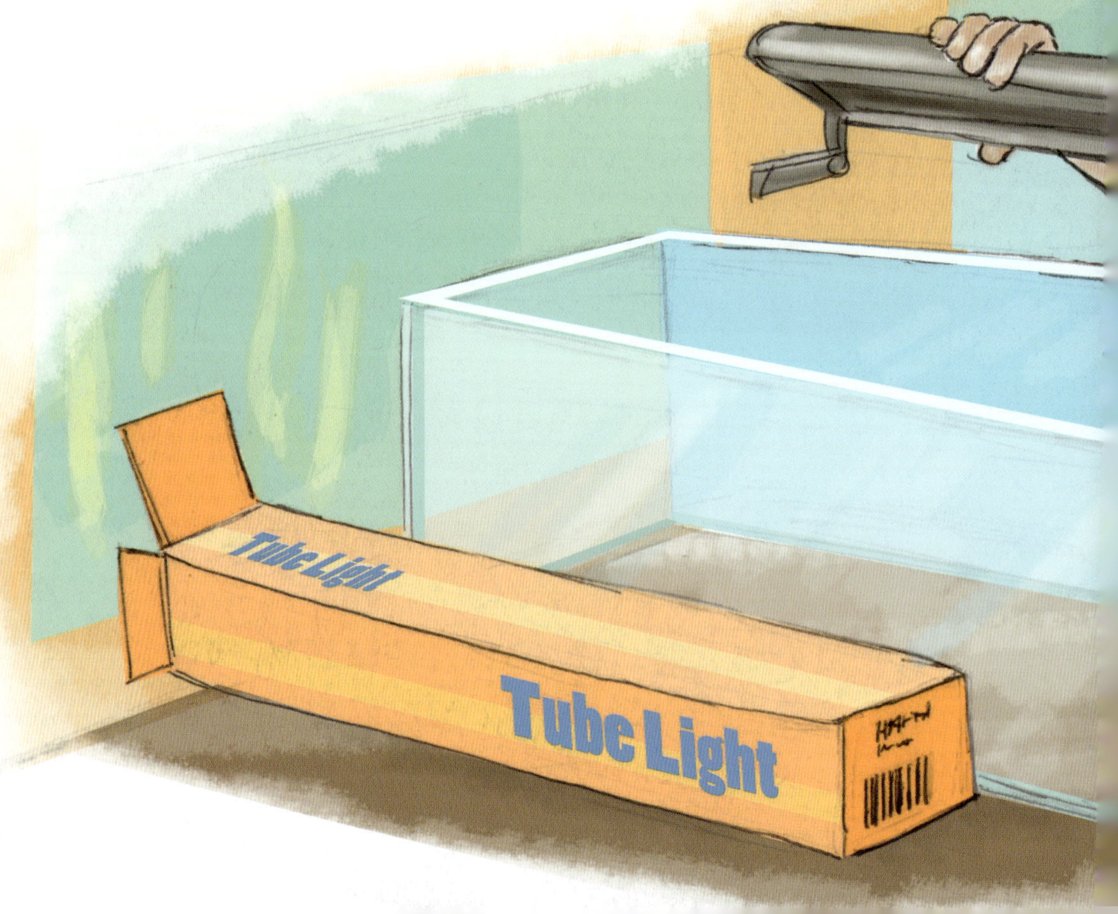

Water Heater

When we got home,
Mum put the tank on a table
in our family room.

I helped her get the aquarium ready
for our pet turtle.

We put the big stones in the tank.
Mum fixed the light to the top.

I was careful when I put in the water.

Mum put the heater in the tank
and turned it on.
Soon, the water was warm.

The next morning,
Mum and I went back to the pet shop.
We looked at all the turtles.
We liked a little turtle with red ears.
I wanted to call him Tiny.

The man in the shop
put a wet paper towel in a small box.
Then, he took Tiny out of the big aquarium
and put him in the box.

Mum got some turtle food
before we left the shop.

She told me turtles eat lots of things.
They eat apples, too.

TURTLE
FOOD
TURTLE
FOOD
TURTLE
FOOD

As soon as we got home,
I put Tiny into the aquarium.

He sat on the stones
under the light to get warm.

Then, he slowly slipped down
into the water.

Mum and I
have wanted a pet turtle
for a long time.

This aquarium is a good home
for Tiny.

TURTLE
FOOD

Glossary

aquarium a tank of water

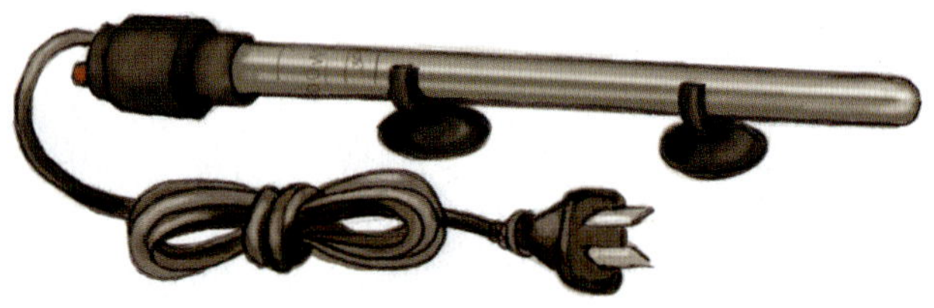

heater a machine for warming water

light a lamp